AF586495

Dialogue between a Muslim and Jerusalem

Dialogue between a Muslim and Jerusalem

The Muslim crusade will not take place for you Jerusalem, since God, through the Koran, commanded us to turn our backs on you.

Saïdou WA Moussa

ISBN: 978-2-9586790-3-3
Printed by Amazon KDP
7,90 €
Dépôt Légal Septembre 2024

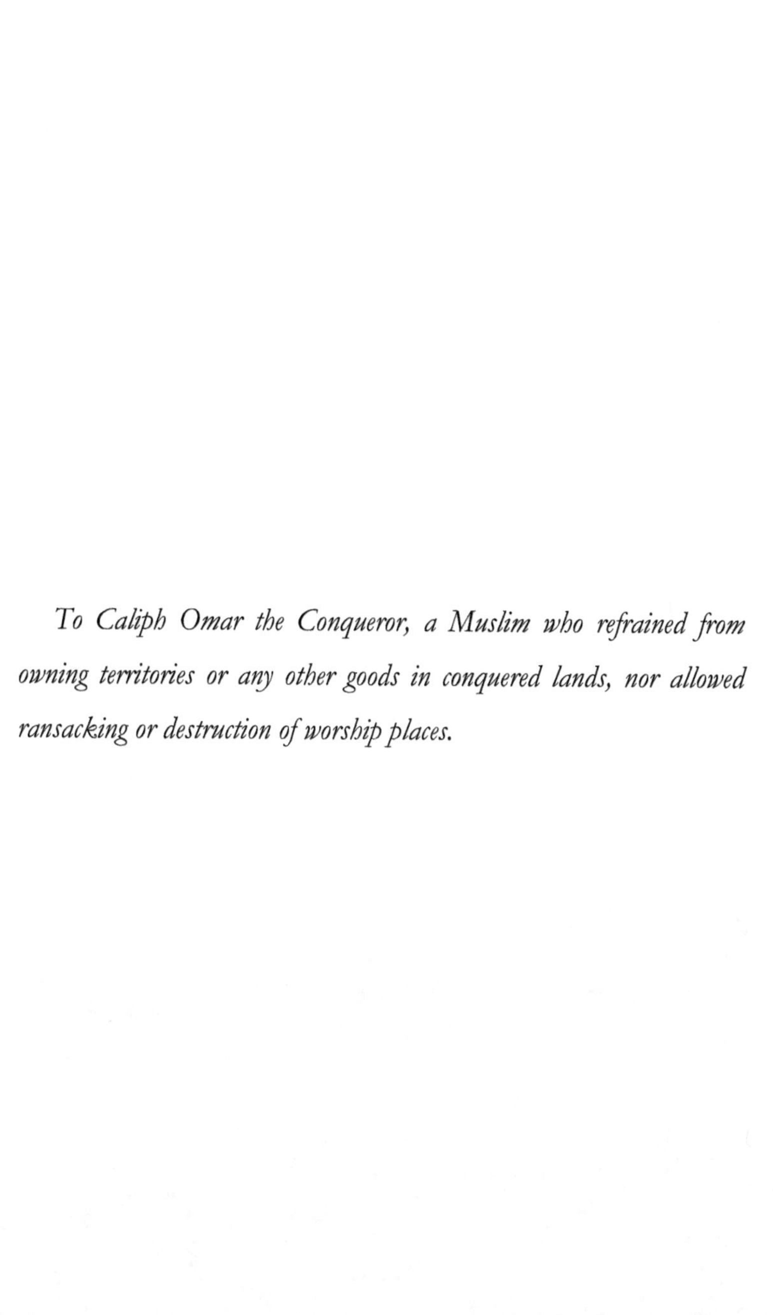

To Caliph Omar the Conqueror, a Muslim who refrained from owning territories or any other goods in conquered lands, nor allowed ransacking or destruction of worship places.

Foreword

Temple Mount, Esplanade of the Mosques, Judaism, Islam, what's the point of all this?

God commands us not to associate Him with anything.

Jerusalem must be demystified and desecrated to preserve life: let's not allow ignorant people to drag the world into a religious war! Verses from the Quran teach us that in the beginning, prayer was destined to Jerusalem. But this was to acknowledge the true Islam believers, those who were to follow the prophet Muhammad when the payer changes towards Mecca.

Therefore, those who call for jihad are totally ignorant of their Book. Muslims who understand what is written in the Quran shall not lead a crusade for Jerusalem.

And to Judaism believers who wish to rebuild the third temple where the Temple of Solomon stood, on the location of the al-Aqsa Mosque: would a temple without the criterium be anything more than just a normal synagogue? Would they lead a crusade for a synagogue?

What can be done to appease passions and prevent confrontations between Jews and Muslims? In the Middle Ages in Andalusia, Jewish scholars, Moses, Maimonides and Judas Halevi accused Christians and Muslims of being pagan worshipers of the wooden cross and of the black stone of Kaaba. What would they think of the children of Israel returning to the land of their ancestors, land they were chased from by the Romans? Two thousand years have passed, and Jerusalem has become a reality and not a dream – Next Year in Jerusalem – today they have become worshipers of the Wall?

Should Maimonides, father of the guide of the lost, return and write a new guide for the lost of Abraham's original monotheism?

A TRIBUTE TO THE SHEPHERD OF PEACE

In memory of Egypt's President Anwar Sadat. Egypt, land of refuge of Abraham during the famine of Canaan; homeland of Hagar the Egyptian, mother of Ishmael and concubine of Abraham; haven for Joseph sold by his brothers to the Ishmaelites and for Jacob and the tribes during the drought and famine once again in Canaan. Egypt, country of birth of Moses, cradle of history and founding myths of Judaism and Israel.

Sadat, the shepherd of peace, whose visit to Israel in 1978 put an end to the state of war between Egypt and Israel. Peace was thus established and prevented war between two brotherly countries for forty-three years, sparing lives on both sides of the border.

*
* *

We have often seen you gaze up and question the sky. So, from now on, we will point you in a direction you will surely approve of. Look towards the Sacred Mosque! And all of you believers, wherever you may be, turn your faces to the same direction! As for those to whom the Book has been given, they know well that it is the truth that has come from the Lord.

And God is not inattentive to what they do (Quran II, 144).

To each an orientation towards which he turns to pray. But it is essential that one competes in the path of righteousness. Wherever you are, God will remind you all of Him. Truly, the power of God is in all things (Quran II, 148).

*
* *

Muslim: Jerusalem, what is the reason for so much passion?

Jerusalem: Is it my fault? Ask the Father, the Son and the Holy Spirit.

Muslim: Ah! The Christian Trinity?

Jerusalem: No, you're mistaken because Jesus and Christianity came after me.

Muslim: Abraham? Ishmael or Isaac? And the one true God?

Jerusalem: No, it is rather the Kaaba, the temple of Mecca which is the doing of Abraham and his son Ishmael (Quran II, 127), who probably wanted to thank God for saving Ishmael and his mother Hagar, when, upon divine injunction, Abraham brought them to the Saudi desert which was to become Mecca. These Muslims! And it must be me, the Jew – Jerusalem – who teaches them the founding myths of Islam?

Muslim: So what? After all, you boast of being the people of the Book, don't you?

Jerusalem: Yes, the Torah, first of the holy Books of monotheism. But don't get me wrong. The God of our ancestors surely gave Moses – Moussa – the Tables of the Law, the Book, at Mount Sinai (Quran II, 53). But to express their beliefs, in Andalusia – the Muslim caliphate in Spain – another Moussa ben Maamoun ben Abdallah El Cordie El Israeli –

Maimonides – as well as other Jewish scholars all wrote in Arabic. Before Haim Yousef Brenner or Ben Yehuda, fathers of modern Hebrew.

Muslim: It is not surprising for an Arab, Moussa Ben Abdallah, to write in Arabic.

Jerusalem: And what do you make of El Israeli? He too, like that of Mount Sinai, is from the tribe of Israel and not from Ishmael.

Muslim: Aw! How you my cousins, my brothers like to argue; debating is part of your culture and has caused you too much harm throughout the ages. It is the reason why so many Talmud books were burnt by the Christians in the Middle Ages. This book nurtures debate and contradiction specific to your culture. Ishmael, Israel, it's all the same, kif-kif! Remove the third letter from the left from both names, or the fourth from the right as we Arabs Is(h)maelites and you Jews, Israelites, write from right to left, and you get the same surname – Is ael=Is ael –, but that's a different story.

Jerusalem: Hey! Why so much hatred from the Ishmaelites towards us Israelites since we are brothers and cousins as you so rightly reminded us? Brothers since our first ancestor, Sem, the son of Noah – Nouha. Thus, you and I are Semites. Our second ancestor was neither Jewish nor Christian, but he was a convinced monotheist and fully dedicated to God. He therefore never belonged to the pagan clan as it is said in your Book, the Koran (III, 67).

Muslim: Come now, try a little harder and you will finally acknowledge the revelations – Christianity and Islam – that came after yours – Judaism – and their prophets, instead of assassinating Jesus or trying to kill Muhammad – Mahomet.

Jerusalem: Unfounded accusations, it's fair game. Placing the three branches of monotheism to compete with each other. It was Rome, a colonialist, polytheist power, occupying the kingdom of Judah, and it's prefect and governor Pontius Pilate along with local auxiliaries, chief priests and the Temple sacerdotal aristocracy who wanted to preserve their interests: the exploitation of the riches of the Temple, the sacrifices, currency activity between the pilgrims and the chief priests and the teachers of the law, as well as the priestly aristocracy. And civil peace for the governor of the Roman Empire. It was them who put Jesus to death. Jesus, they considered as a dangerous agitator, a revolutionary who threatened their interests, and not as a prophet since the Judean aristocracy of the Temple ignored that Jesus of Nazareth was a prophet as he himself recalled before he was killed: "Then Jesus said: "Father, forgive them, for they do not know what they are doing." (Luc 23, 34). Because for the aristocracy of the Temple, Jesus of Nazareth was nothing but the leader of a subversive Jewish sect, like so many others at the time. But it was also a prophecy that came true: "Truly, the son of man goeth, as it was determined: but woe unto that man by whom he is betrayed!" (Luc 22, 22) So, Christians and Muslims, please read and interpret your texts correctly and stop accusing me of deicide or persecuting me and wanting to exterminate me.

Muslim: And Jerusalem, are you going to deny the attempted assassination of the prophet of Islam by the rabbis of Yathrib – Medina?

Jerusalem: Random accusations, ingratitude! remember Ishmaelites, Muslims, that it is the three Jewish tribes – the Banus Qaïnuqa, the Banus n-Nadir and the Banus Quraïza, monotheists of Yathrib (Medina) – who brought you back on the right path of the monotheism of the fathers and got you out of paganism, or pre-Islamic Jahiliya, that you had sunk into(Ad, Thamud, Amalekites…). Remember, Muslims of the world, that it was these Judaic tribes who welcomed, protected and made a pact with Muhammad – May God Bless Him – against the Arabs, Ishmaelites, polytheist Meccans. It is rather a council of Mecca notables, who saw in Muhammad – MGBH – a dangerous agitator, like Jesus with the priests of the temple. It was these Mecca notables who actually wanted to assassinate the prophet of Islam. A group of young nobles of Mecca were to surprise him in his sleep and kill him, but the prophet miraculously escaped assassination. Hence the flight, or hijra and the exodus towards Yathrib (Medina) – the Hegira in September 622 – of Muhammad – MGBH – who was not yet known as a prophet.

Along with Abu Bakr, they fled from their enemies and, with their companions, hid in a cave where a spider wove its web and blocked the entrance to trick and mislead their pursuers.

In Mecca, the prophet of Islam benefited from the tribal protection and solidarity – all the Hashemites, especially his uncles Abu Talib, al-Abbas, Abu Lahad whose wife sewered thorns after the passage of the prophet. Nevertheless, the uncles remained faithful to ancestral paganism, against the Meccan polytheists, Abu Djahl and the Umayyad Abu Sufyan. The latter and his children were to become Muslims and great conquerors of Islam.

From conquered Syria, Damascus will become the capital of the Muslim empire, ruled by the Umayyad dynasty.

But the prophet was unwelcomed in places others than in the city of Mecca. In the south-east of Mecca, among the Taqif of Taif, the prophet was chased out of the polytheist Arab city amid jeers and stones thrown by the children encouraged by the notables.

Once again, I am teaching you your history, to remind you that the fierce enemies of emerging Islam were not the Jewish tribes of the oasis of Khaybar or Medina, but indeed Arabs, Ishmaelites like the prophet.

Medina became a refuge and rear base for the reconquest of Mecca, the ancestral holy capital of the Ishmaelites because of the presence of the Kaaba built by Abraham and his first son Ishmael. And while Abraham and Ishmael were raising the foundations of the Kaaba, they said: "Our Lord, accept this work from us! You are the Hearer, You are the Knowing!" (the Koran, II, 127). But what was to become of the Kaaba, a pagan shrine of pre-Islamic Arabia…

After the triumph of Islam in Arabia and throughout the world, Mecca once again became monotheist and holy capital of Islam, and the Kaaba once again became a monotheistic temple of Muslim pilgrimage as it was predicted in the Koran: "Then, We made the House a resort and a sanctuary for people, saying 'Take the spot where Abraham stood as your place of prayer'. And We commanded Abraham and Ishmael; 'Purify My House for those who walk around it, who stay here, and those who bow and prostrate themselves in worship'." (Quran II, 125).

It was these Judaizing, monotheist communities from a polytheist Medina and the mouhadjroun, a handful of companions of the prophet from Mecca who welcomed the preacher Muhammad – May God Bless Him – and not the mounafiqin, hypocrite Ishmaelites, Arabic disbelievers in the words of the prophet, or the radical opponent of Muhammad – MGBH – and the new religion: the hanif Abou Amir ar-Rahib, who preferred to leave his city of Medina for pagan Mecca in order not to live with or convert to the new religion – Islam.

Muslim: Provocation and controversy again!

Jerusalem: Simple reminder, just a clarification to your mortifying accusations – accusations of deicide of Christians and Muslims against me, an Israelite. Whereas it is God himself who called Jesus back to Him. Then God said "O Jesus! I will take you and raise you up to Me. I will deliver you from those who disbelieve and elevate your followers above the disbelievers until the Day of Judgment. Then to Me you will all return, and I will settle all your disputes." (Quran III, 55).

Muslim: Let's stop counting sheep. Not our Bedouin ancestor's sheep nor the one Abraham sacrificed in place of Ishmael. Tell us: Who are you, Jerusalem?

Jerusalem: I will tell you who I am. But allow me to rectify, the sacrificed was not Ishmael but rather Isaac.

Muslim: Such a wiseguy little brother! These Israelites! I, an Ishmaelite, was thirteen years old (Genesis XVII, 24, 25, 26) when you were barely born (GXXI, 5), and you claim to have carried (GXXII, 6) the wood to light the holocaust fire? Or would you dare call our Father a liar, Jerusalem? For in the Holy Book, our Father gives thanks to God for having blessed Him with Ishmael and Isaac, despite his great age: first, I, Ishmael, then you, Isaac: "All praise is for You my Lord who has blessed me with Ishmael and Isaac in my old age!

My Lord is indeed the Hearer of all my prayers!" (Quran XIV, 39).

Jerusalem: Muslims acknowledge the holy books (Quran II, 136; Koran III, 3) which precede them, and which inspired them – the Torah and the Gospel – but do not read them: they only do so when it suits them. But this time, you seem to be right big brother Ishmael! There is a logic. The Ishmaelite, proud and vain, who always wants to be right, is not necessarily dominating. I, an Israelite, recognize that Ishmael is the elder brother of Isaac, and it is in reality Ishmael, the elder brother, who is the Sacrificed.

Muslim: Why would I read the Torah, and the Gospel since the Koran summarizes and completes them? But when I read them, I will do so with caution and vigilance because of the negligence of the scribes, the perversity of the text-correctors, who added or removed at will, their bias as Judeo-Christians. They had just been excluded forever from Judaism by the orthodox Pharisees and had issues to settle with them. The Gospels of Matthew and John – the early Jewish Christians – will subsequently establish a war of slander against Orthodox Jews or Jews in general for centuries, among other accusations that of a deicidal people or that against Ishmael: "He (Ishmael) will be like a wild donkey; his hand will be against all, and the hand of all will be against him; and he will live opposite all his brothers" (G XVI; 12); or the Gospel which clearly intended on sowing discord between Ishmael and Isaac on the issue of the sacrifice: "God said to Abraham: Take your son, your only son, whom you love – Isaac – and go to the region of Moriah. Sacrifice him there as a burnt offering on one of the mountains I will show you" (G XXII; 2).

And why did the scribes and correctors add Isaac after having clearly specified "your son, your only son, our father could not have sacrificed you since you were not yet born"?

Jerusalem: Alright, although this doesn't happen very often, I confirm, big brother Ishmael. But you must do the same when you Muslims read the Quran. Do not interpret it like the Christian scribes, correctors or exegetes.

Muslim: Now that we have settled our family differences – deicide, attempted assassination of Mohammed, birthright, the sacrificed… tell us instead who you are, Jerusalem. And stop Judaizing yourself by saying you are Jewish and Israelite.

Jerusalem: I admit my origins are not Israelite but rather Jebusite or Jebusian (G XV, 21), a Canaanite tribe.

Muslim: How did you become an Israelite? Jewish? Judean?

Jerusalem: I was called Jebus and was conquered by King David of Judea: an Israelite (chronicles XI; 4,5,6,7,8,9) from Hebron, capital of the kingdom of Judas. I then became the city of David, Yerushalayim, Jerusalem: Israelite, Judean because David was an Israelite from the tribe of Judah – one f the twelve tribes of Jacob-Israel – mentioned throughout the surahs and verses of the Quran.

Muslim: Oh! The same King David mentioned in the Quran for his fight against Goliath? "So they defeated their enemies by God's will, and David killed Goliath. And God blessed David with kingship and wisdom and taught him what He willed. Had God not repelled a group of people by the might of another, corruption would have dominated the earth. But God is gracious to all" (Quran II; 251). Is he the father?

Jerusalem: Yes, he is the second Hebrew king, chosen by God for the Israelites (chronicles XI; 1, 2, 3), because God deposed Saul, the first king for having questioned the divine power (chronicles X; 13, 14).

Muslim: Abraham was Hebrew not David. There you want the patriarch to be an Israelite, while he was neither Jew nor Christian as the Koran recalls: "Abraham was neither a Jew nor a Christian; he was a convinced monotheist, wholly devoted to God. He therefore never belonged to the pagans'clan" (Quran III, 67).

Jerusalem: Nor was he a Muslim for the revealed Books and religions are subsequent to Abraham the patriarch.

Muslim: And why you, Jerusalem and no other place? Why not David's conquest, Canaan or Hebron, which was the capital of David's kingdom since he was already king of Judea?

Jerusalem: It was for neutrality between the twelve tribes of Israel. As I have told you before, I was Jebus from the Canaanite tribe of the Jebusites, not an Israelite. But Judea was the kingdom of only two of the twelve tribes of Israel. To avoid any rivalry between the twelve tribes and for freedom of worship, King David made me the capital of all tribes, of a united Israelite kingdom.

Muslim: When did that happen?

Jerusalem: It dates back to about a thousand years before Jesus Christ and Christianity. Two hundred and fifty years after the Israelites entered Canaan, after the flight from Egypt and the Exodus. The Quran also relates the Exodus and the Israelites'entrance into Canaan.

Muslim: So, in the beginning you were Canaanite, the land promised to Abraham by his one God (G XII;7). Canaan, miraculously conquered by the Israelites after their flight from Egypt, became the Kingdom of Israel. After being taken by

King David from the Jebusites, a Canaanite tribe… this is how Yerushalayim, Rushalinum or Jerusalem was born. The capital of the unified Jewish kingdoms.

Jerusalem: Absolutely! Since at that time neither Christianity nor Islam were yet revealed. Their prophets unknown, just simple men… A story between Canaanites since the Israelites had returned from exile – Jacob and his family were Canaanites when the seventy members of his family joined Joseph in Egypt – which lasted four hundred years in Egypt and became Canaanites again. After they left Egypt and the Exodus, they conquered the Canaanite territory thus joining the other Israelites who had remained on site in Canaan, as God had promised Abraham… or a story between Canaanites and Israelites. You see, dear Muslim, Israel as the world knows it is an Israeli invention. Because, as long as the Israelites were not interested in Jebus, it was an ordinary city, unknown to all. There is a good reason for the rest of humanity to call us the people – Israel – inventor of something. This stokes attraction, jealousy, hatred and misfortunes against me, an Israelite, but that's another story.

Muslim: Again, arrogance and provocation, I don't want to argue. So, you said it was King David, the father, who chose you to be the capital of the one and only Jewish kingdom, Israel. But whose father is David?

Jerusalem: King David is the father of King Solomon – Souleiman in the Koran – his successor to the throne. Solomon is the one responsible for the passion monotheists have for me, Jerusalem.

Muslim: Oh, I see. Solomon is the son we are talking about? Why would he be responsible for the passion if not the quarrel, or God forbid, a fratricidal war between monotheists over you, Jerusalem?

Jerusalem: Because Solomon, the son, wanted to revive the tradition of the ancestors who built altars or sanctuaries dedicated to the one God. "The Lord appeared to Abraham and said, 'to your offspring I will give this land' so he built an altar there to the Lord who appeared to him. From there he went on to Bethel and pitched his tent. There he built an altar to the Lord" (G XII; 7, 8).

Muslim: And Solomon built an altar, a sanctuary in thanks to the God of Abraham? For what blessing?

Jerusalem: Perhaps for the divine promise to Abraham of a land for him and his descendants, a promise that came true with the conquest of Canaan undertaken by Joshua – the Bible and the Koran speak of this conquest. It was carried on by the judges Jephthah, Gideon, Samson and finalized by David, all descendants of the twelve tribes of Israel, Isaac and Abraham.

Muslim: And what does the God of Abraham have to do with this conquest?

Jerusalem: The obstacles were such that it was an impossible undertaking without divine intervention. But that's another story.

Muslim: And Solomon built an altar to thank Baal and Ashtaroth, Canaanite gods?

Jerusalem: No, rather a temple to shelter the Ark of the Covenant and a house of prayer to commune with the God of Abraham: the One who delivered the Hebrews, or Israelites, from slavery in Egypt, and who offered Canaan to His nation as he had promised Abraham (Genesis XII,7) and Jacob-Israel (Genesis XXVIII, 13).

Muslim: His nation? Does God have a specific nation? And I suppose its name is Israel?

Jerusalem: Yes, nation of God, blessed and loved, because God delivered Israel from slavery in Egypt, offered them the Tables of the Law at Mount Sinai, and brought them back to Canaan, the land of their ancestors Abraham and Isaac.

Muslim: You associator! God is not begotten and has not begotten. He created Adam, the father and we are all children of Adam, God's creation. So, Jerusalem – Israel – do not return to the Canaanite syncretism of the Israelites, barely out of the desert. Is your God that of Abraham or the Canaanite gods?

Jerusalem: Absolutely not. I am a monotheist, as in the beginning with our father Abraham. It is you, descendants of Ishmael, who broke the promise made to Abraham to always keep monotheism as the only religion.

Muslim: But wasn't there already an Israelite temple in Shiloh in Bethel, dedicated to the God of Israel? Why another temple in Jerusalem?

Jerusalem: Perhaps you mean the early tents which housed the Ark of the Covenant during our wanderings. Let's recap: King David conquered me when I was called Jebus. He made me the capital of his kingdom because I didn't belong to any of the twelve tribes of Israel, much like the American capital, Washington, which doesn't belong to any of the fifty-one states of the United States of America. Some say that the founding fathers were inspired by King David's idea of a neutral capital. For this neutrality, King David transferred the Holy Ark to Jerusalem in order to make it a spiritual capital as well as a political capital.

Neutral, so that all the tribes of Israel could come and commune freely with the One God of Abraham.

Muslim: What is this Ark of the Covenant? How does it fit in our story?

Jerusalem: Don't be so impulsive, keep calm. Remember the Surah II; 53 of the Koran: These are the Tables of the Law given By God to Moses at Mount Sinai. Remember what I told you earlier. Law which must govern the daily life of every Israelite, and later the reveled Christianity and Islam, of every monotheist during their life on this earth.

Muslim: Since Moses met God on Mount Sinai, Why didn't Solomon build his temple there? Like it is the case for al-Aqsa that was built where Muhammad set out on his nightly journey to the heavens to meet God, or for the Holy Sepulcher built where Jesus Christ was born again and rose to heaven to join God, as the verse mentioned above reminds us.

Jerusalem: I forgot to tell you, I who was first to receive the Book, that on the site of the temple God appeared to Abraham the patriarch, on the rock of Isaac's sacrifice, replacing the latter with a ram. And the resurrection of Jesus Christ, as well as the journey of the prophet of Islam, both took place in Jerusalem because of the presence of the Temple, the Rock, the Tables of the Law placed in the Temple. And why, may I ask you again, did this journey not start from Mecca or Medina, or the resurrection of Jesus Christ in Nazareth?

Muslim: What confusion, Jerusalem! Father, Son, Holy Spirit, Tables of the Law, Ark of the Covenant… and now you talk about the rock where Ishmael was almost sacrificed by our Father. I thought the debate on our family differences was closed since you admitted I am the sacrificed one.

This is the reason why the Dome of the Mosque of Omar, or al-Aqsa, is built above the Rock and called the Dome of the Rock. But isn't the rock of the sacrifice located in the land of Moriah rather than in Jerusalem?

Jerusalem: No confusion at all! It is only your lack of wisdom and patience, Ishmaelite. The Gospel describes your impulsiveness well, remember the writings of the Christian scribes.

David, the father, created Jerusalem when he conquered The Jebusian city, Jebus, and it became the city of David or Jerusalem. Solomon, the son, built a temple to house God's gift to Moses, the Tables of the Law, and to welcome all who pray and commune with the God of Abraham. This is my answer to your first question: ask the Father, the Son and the Holy Spirit, or God – David, Solomon and the Holy Spirit, The God of Abraham. By placing the Tables of the Law – God's gift to Israel and proof of the encounter between Moses and God on Mount Sinai – in the Israelite temple it became an oratory, a landmark of the one and only God. Not detectable, not comparable to any of His creations, nor associable. The presence of Abraham the patriarch on earth for all those who avail themselves of him, who identify themselves and claim to be the heirs of Jerusalem. Since the other two encounters were to start from Jerusalem – the resurrection of Jesus Christ and the nocturnal journey of Mohammed... Although in the beginning, Jerusalem was an idea, an invention created by the children of Israel.

Muslim: So, this temple is the reason why you cause so much passion between Jews and Muslims today. And why, after the destruction of this temple in 586 BC by

Nebuchadnezzar, Mesopotamian king, did Solomon's successors rebuild the temple, object of so much passion, discord and wars between the spiritual children of Abraham?

Jerusalem: How could the successors of Solomon who rebuilt the second temple have known I would arouse so much passion? At the time, Jerusalem was only Jewish. Christianity and Islam had not yet been revealed. It had to be this way. It is the fight between monotheism and polytheism initiated by Abraham the monotheist and Nimrud the polytheist in Mesopotamia. According to Muslim tradition, Abraham was a Mesopotamian just like King Nimrud before becoming a Canaanite.

Muslim: So, it's the same fight all over again, thirteen centuries after Abraham's departure from Mesopotamia. A fight between the descendants of Abraham, faithful to ancestral monotheism as the children of Israel promised their father on his deathbed (Quran II, 133), and the descendant of the polytheist tyrant Nimrud, the new Mesopotamian despot Nebuchadnezzar?

Jerusalem: Absolutely. Shortly after the destruction of the first temple, God made Cyrus the Great, the Persian king, triumph over Nebuchadnezzar. Thus, The God of Abraham punished Nebuchadnezzar and allowed the epic of monotheism to follow its destiny through the Children of Israel and Judaism.

Muslim: This explains the children of Israel's determination to remain monotheists and rebuild the Temple, even without the Ark of the Covenant, and to reaffirm their attachment and loyalty to the one God of the fathers who saved them so many times? One can see you are not ungrateful, Jerusalem.

Jerusalem: Yes! For without the Temple, symbol dedicated to the God of the fathers, perhaps the children of Jerusalem would have succumbed to Canaanite paganism. It is like a physical reminder of God… Just like the children of Ishmael succumbed to Jahiliya or paganism in Arabia, before returning to monotheism with the advent of Islam and its prophet Muhammad – MGBH.

Muslim: And this conflict between monotheism and polytheism is recurrent. Half a millennium later, another polytheistic empire from far away, the Roman Empire, destroyed the Temple once again and put an end to the Jewish State, the kingdom of Judah. Why did the passion for Jerusalem not disappear with the destruction of the second temple by Titus? And with the disappearance of the Tables of the Law, if they hadn't disappeared with the first destruction?

Jerusalem: This passion for Jerusalem remains. It survives in the memory of generations of Judean descendants of the diaspora. And on the inside, because temple Judaism was replaced by synagogal Judaism and Jewish Jerusalem gave way to a holy Jerusalem once again. But this time with another monotheism with the advent of Jesus Christ and Christianity… and later, with the advent of another monotheism, Islam. With the nocturnal journey of the prophet of Islam – a dream like Jacob's Ladder, or tangible – Jerusalem will become holy for the third time, hence the name of the thrice-holy city.

Muslim: And so it was a miracle, the nocturnal journey which took place where the Temple of Solomon was located, which is the origin of the passion of Muslims for Jerusalem?

Jerusalem: Indeed it was. In addition, after the advent of Islam and its conquests, the Caliph Omar revived memories by cleaning the site soiled by the polytheist Roman occupants who had built a polytheist temple where the first and second Jewish monotheistic temples stood. The Romans became monotheist Christians after the advent of Jesus and Christianity. As new masters of the country they chose to create their own founding myth of their religion. So they built their own altar, their temple on the site of the martyr, Golgotha, where Jesus Christ was buried. The Church of the Holy Sepulcher is there to remind generations of Christians of Jesus, his martyrdom and his resurrection. The site the Christianized Romans abandoned became a dump. The Caliph Omar had it cleaned and built a Mosque on the foundations. These were the foundations where the temples of Solomon and Herod I the Great were located, before Abd al-Malik built the Mosque of Omar, or al-Aqsa. For it is from this exact place that the prophet of Islam started his journey to the heavens, as I have recalled before, dear Muslim brother-cousin.

Muslim: Hence the passion and attachment of Muslims for Jerusalem?

Jerusalem: Exactly! And I can understand them, because after Caliph Omar, Muslims were the faithful guardians of the monotheist site. They even accepted that the Jews who had been banished by the Romans return to Jerusalem.

Muslim: Not only were we, Muslims, the guardians of this site, formerly the Temple Mount which became the esplanade of the Mosques, but we also fought absurd, fratricidal monotheist wars for you, Jerusalem. As a matter of fact, the wars between monotheistic and polytheistic Jews, Babylonians and Romans gave way for centuries to wars between monotheists, Christians and Muslims, who thought they believed in the same God… God who was meant to unite them, and not lead them to fight each other.

Jerusalem: You Muslims talk about absurd wars of the past. So why do you want to start a new conflict with another monotheism, Judaism? Can't you love and cherish Jerusalem without wanting to possess it, since you already have Mecca and Medina as spiritual shrines?

Muslim: Apparently, I am not the only one to suffer from amnesia nor the only one who doesn't learn from the past! It is always the moment's strongest who wants to possess you exclusively, Jerusalem. And he wants to submit his opponent or even banish him… as you were by Hadrian. This is the intention of King Netanyahu who wants to take over the legacy of David and Solomon, while forgetting that Abraham's God sent two prophets – Jesus Christ and Mohammed – binding them to Jerusalem. And this to re-give the hand to an exhausted Judaism in order to monotheize other peoples. Are we going to agree with the German pilgrim Dominican friar, who said regarding Jerusalem in 1480-1483: "The city is in a state of desolation… the unfortunate Jerusalem has suffered, still suffers, and will suffer of more sieges, damage, destruction and terror than any other city in the world."?

Jerusalem: So what do you suggest, Muslim brother, since the dispute is between the two of us, Jews and Muslims? Because Christians in the Holy Land and in the East are on the verge of extinction.

Muslim: It has always been the same pattern as in Jerusalem, at all times and in all places: the strongest of the moment takes possession of the worship places of those defeated and adapts them to his cult. For example, Muslims added the Mihrab which indicates the direction of Mecca for prayer and not Jerusalem, and the Minbar, where the imam preaches. The bell tower becomes a minaret for the call to prayer. This is what happened with the Church in Cordoba after the Muslim conquest of Spain. And, with a few exceptions, there was destruction… As in Jerusalem in the year 1009, when the Fatimid Caliph of Egypt Al Hakim tore down the Holy Sepulcher and triggered the Christian crusades from the West to free Jerusalem. Conversely, after the Reconquista, King Ferdinand of Castile consecrated the mosque of Cordoba as a church and transformed the minaret into a bell tower. The Church of Saint Sophia in Istanbul in Turkey, built on the site of an ancient polytheist temple which became a mosque after the Ottoman conquest, a museum with Christian visitors… But the most surprising ancient example of this tolerance is the mosque of Damascus or Omayyad mosque. Originally, it was a pagan temple dedicated to Jupiter. It was transformed into a church after the Arab conquest and the Muslims shared it with the Christians, half serving as a church and the other half as a mosque. Perhaps, if the Romans hadn't destroyed the Temple, Caliph Omar would not have built a mosque in its place, since he prevented Muslims from destroying the Holy Sepulcher and forbade them to pray or settle there.

Jerusalem: Again, I ask you: Why can't you be passionate and attached to Jerusalem without wanting to possess her?

Muslim: Why not? Remember the verses we mentioned in the beginning of our dialogue: God has ordered us to turn to another direction to pray (Quran II, 142, 143). God commands us to turn and face the Sacred Mosque of the Mecca for prayer (Quran II, 144). So, when praying on the esplanade of the mosques or of the temple, Muslim believers have their backs to al-Aqsa Mosque, as if they were saying to the idolatrous of the wall: we have guarded and protected your wall where the temple of Solomon stood, during the 1,400 years of your exile. We are now returning it to you because God orders that wherever we may be, we turn our face towards the oratory of Abraham, towards the Kaaba. Why argue over some wall since "Everyone has their own direction towards which they turn to pray. It is essential to seek to surpass one another in doing good. Because wherever you may be, God will bring you to Him. Truly, the power of God is in all things" (Quran II, 148)? According to this verse from the Quran, God cannot be located, not in a temple, nor in a church or in a mosque, since his power extends to everything. However, we are not attentive to divine signs.

I am a Muslim, and the oratory of Abraham chosen for me by God as the direction towards which I must turn to pray – instead of Jerusalem towards which I initially turned – prevails and fulfills me, since it is God's will. "We only fixed the direction to which you initially turned to distinguish those who will follow the prophet from those who turned away from him…" (Quran II; 143). So I will follow the prophet and not turn away from him.

Obviously, I will not shed any blood for you, Jerusalem.

And the Muslim crusade will not take place for you, Jerusalem.

But Jerusalem, if Omar's mosque or al-Aqsa was to be removed from the site where Solomon's temple was built and replaced by a temple without the Holy Ark, would you still be a holy city for the three monotheisms?

Jerusalem: Yes, it would because it is there that the two founding myths were born. The resurrection of Jesus for Christianity and the nocturnal celestial journey of Muhammad towards the heavens for Islam. And the Tables of the Law were there. God united the three monotheistic religions together in one place, in Jerusalem.

Muslim: Without the Holy Ark, and Jesus not being born there nor buried there since he was resurrected and rose to heaven, and relieved of the al-Aqsa Mosque which recalls the journey of the prophet of Islam, Jerusalem would not arouse such passion. She would become Jebu once again, an ordinary capital alike so many others around the world... And have you forgotten Solomon's prophecy?

"When your people, Israel, fall before the enemy, because they have sinned against you, if they return and praise your Name, pray and beseech you in this Temple, you in heaven listen and forgive the sin of your people Israel and lead them back to the land you gave their fathers.

As the foreigner who does not belong to your people Israel but has come from a distant land for your Name's sake – for they will hear of your great Name and your mighty hand and your outstretched arm – when they come to pray in this Temple, then hear them from heaven your dwelling place and grant all their requests so that all the peoples of the world recognize your Name." (I Kings VIII, 41-42, Solomon's speech when inaugurating the Temple).

Are you not going against the prophecy, Jerusalem, by wanting to become a Judaic Israelite city, while through the prophet Solomon, God had predicted that Jerusalem was to be a city for all monotheistic peoples of the world, a city with a universal vocation? Didn't God tell the prophet Solomon to proclaim it?

Was the inaugural speech an announcement of the advent of the prophets Jesus Christ and Muhammad – MGBH –, of Christianity and Islam?

As the Quran recalled…

Remember also what Jesus, the son of Mary, said: "O children of Israel, indeed I am the messenger of God to you confirming what came before me of the Torah and bringing good tidings of a messenger to come after me, whose name is Ahmad." But when he came to them with clear evidence, they said: "This is obvious magic!" (Quran 61,6).

***

David, the father, and Solomon, the son, must be turning over in their graves, they who, by divine will, wanted a capital for the unity of the tribes of Israel – David, a spiritual capital – Solomon, who built an oratory dedicated to the God of Abraham and proof of the Tables of the Law, gift of the one God to monotheists entrusted to the people of Israel.

This people were witness at Mount Sinai, therefore Jerusalem is the city of monotheism, a universal vocation open to the three branches of Abrahamic monotheism.

Whereas Mecca and Medina are exclusive holy places specific to Islam and Muslims, and Rome a holy place reserved for Christianity and Christians… While Jerusalem has become by divine will a reminder to monotheists that the advent of the three religions and the passion they arouse in us must not make us forget the essential: the "Oneness" of Hashem, God and Allah. Communicating with Him must not be a cause of division, confrontation, war and death, but rather of unity, dialogue peace and life.

And Saladin, the unifier of Islam who fought the Crusades for over ten years, left a testament message to his mother and for all mankind before passing away: "Men must fight no more. Tell them, Oumy. There is only one God. Allah, the God of the Christians, that of the Jews are all the same God. The one and universal God who was not begotten and who did not generate. There was Abraham, Moses, Jesus, then Mohammed, and there is only one religion, that of this one God. This is the truth. I believe in my soul that God blew in your womb."

Whoever has the privilege by God's will of possessing this city, must know he is only the guardian of a holy place open to all – Judaism, Christianity, Islam.

Let us meditate on these two verses from the Quran:

Say: "O People of the Book! Let us come to common terms: that we will worship none but God, associate none with Him, nor take one another as lords instead of God". But if they turn away, then say, "Bear witness that we have submitted to God alone." (Quran 364).

So Jerusalem must be, or symbolize, this divine unity, the unity of monotheists, a single God for humanity, in a single city… This is possible if we act with intelligence. Jerusalem must be the city of concord not of discord. The city of unity and not of division. The city of human fraternity. The city of peace and not the city of war.

Amen.

About the Author

Saïdou WA Moussa is a Comorian emigrant, cleaning technician by profession.

After a baccalaureate equivalence, he spent two years at the Medical Faculty of Nice but failed at the passing examination.

He then followed night classes and obtained a degree in management at the Faculty of Economics in Nice. He left this diploma in a drawer to continue his job as cleaning technician until he retired nearly two years ago.

He was motivated to write this text by the cynicism of number of politicians and political organizations from Arab-Muslim and Israeli countries who exploit religion in the Arab Israeli conflict, to remind them that a place of prayer – the al-Aqsa mosque, formerly the site of the Temple of Solomon – must not divide or be an area of division.

Mixing politics and religion prevents from finding a solution to this conflict and has been bereaving Israeli and Palestinian families every day for a long time.

The author hopes that by addressing both peoples, his writings will soothe hearts and souls.

Because the One God of Abraham made them brothers who must learn to live together… or die together, "like idiots" as Martin Luther King said…

My special thanks to:

Emmanuelle, Hélène, Marie-Pierre and the entire team of "Ecrire un Livre Accrocheur" (How to write a catchy book).

Azrate, for the Internet part.

Clémentine, Iris, Tulcy who introduced me to the Bible.

André who taught me that Hebrew was written like Arabic, from right to left. I read somewhere Ben Gurion's reply to Leon Blum when the latter told him he was French, socialist and Jewish, and Ben Gurion replied ironically that Hebrew was written from right to left so Leon Blum was Jewish, socialist and French.

Boulares, my first critic of the digital book, who pointed out to me that the reader was lost because I used the initials of the characters in the dialogue instead of the full names, Jerusalem and Muslim.

www.ingramcontent.com/pod-product-compliance
Lightning Source LLC
LaVergne TN
LVHW052108160826
845678LV00015B/3438